For my sister, Pat.

These Memories we do share.

First printed in 2016.
Reprinted 2017.
©2017. PA Daw
© 2017. Liberty Royale P/L

The inspiration for this book comes from time spent with great Australian bushman, stockman and drover, Douglas James Scobie (1910 – 1991).

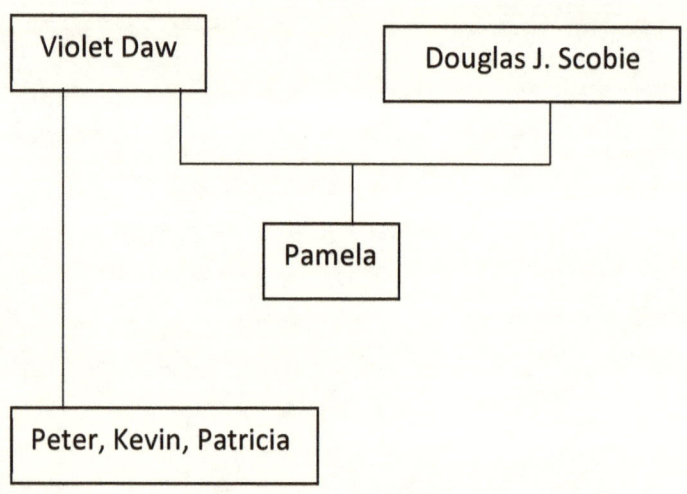

*Each page is a memory, an experience.*

*All verse, history, and experiences are written by Peter A. Daw.*

The Birdsville Track is very arid country between the Simpson Desert and Sturt's Stony Desert. Artesian Bores provide a permanent water source that enabled the cattle and Drovers to travel the length of the Track, from South-West Queensland to the livestock markets in South Australia. Many people have perished here.

The Birdsville Track has recently become a popular tourist attraction, but being so isolated, traversing the harsh country without due care can mean life or death for the inexperienced.

The story *Battlers and Bushmen* is a collection of memories and experiences of a Birdsville Track stockman: growing up and working on the Track during the 1950s and 1960s.

The story provides a richly descriptive account of one man's journey being 'on the run'- the term given for people who spend their days mustering, living in Stock Camps, and sleeping under the stars.

About thirty miles up the Track from Marree is the Dingo Fence, and outside the fence it's open country.
This is where a lot of great Bushmen's stories come from.
Australia had a Cattle Disease Eradication Program which required, among other things, that all properties had to be fenced.
During this time, big changes were taking place: Road trains had taken over, and hence, no more drovers. For cattle work on the stations, light four wheel drives and motorbikes did the job.

All the old Bushmen and horses have gone.

This maybe amongst the last of the stories told.

§§§§§§

Back in Fifty-four,
I told the teacher 'I will not be here anymore'.
'Tomorrow you will be back'.
'No I am heading up the Birdsville Track'.

At fourteen the old bushman came to me,
He said, 'At school you can stay.'
'Or come bush and learn things our way'.

On the train to Marree we did go.
Through Pichi Richi Pass was very slow.
Being young and impatient it did seem a long way,
Heading to my new home where I would stay.

Into Marree at last.
Stepping on to the platform,
All one could see;
Was a pub, post office and shop,
That was the lot.
This is going to be my home.
I felt all alone.

Leaving Marree and heading up the track,
I knew it would be a long time;
Before coming back.
There was no grass or stock about,
The country was in drought.

Out through the first gate,
Then the Frome,
On the way to our new home.

At Dulkaninna we met a family named Bell,
In time, they would be our friends we could tell.
On to Etadunna that night to stay,
Such nice people; helpful in every way.

Past Copperamanna Bore,
Through Coopers Creek,
Over a big sand hill called Oldfield's Leap,
Onto a long stony flat,
In the distance, what we all saw,
Was the homestead called Mulka Store.

On arrival at Mulka Store,
We found a large old homestead.
The building was made of limestone and pug,
This is lime, clay and fibre made into mud.

In the bathroom, there were no taps,
The floors did not have any mats.
We knew it would be tough,
This was very rough.
We made it a nice home to relax and be,
Happy to have friends and family come to see.

It was one of the worst droughts,
We did not have any money or stock,
I can tell you it was a hard lot.
We poisoned dingoes with baits,
To get money for their scalps;
This put food on our plates.

Drovers started coming our way,
Water for their cattle they had to pay.
Three pence per head,
Helped keep us fed.

Then having a few pounds more,
We bought groceries from the wholesalers,
To sell in the store.

The rains came.
We were now Mulka Cattle Station.
The transformation was so great,
We could now have a good life eating steak.

The first vehicle we had at Mulka Store,
Was an old Dodge Flying Four.
It was a city green grocer's cart.
We had to have something for a start.

It had a hot busted exhaust under the floor,
The Old Lady complained her feet were burning.
'I'm not going out in that thing anymore.'

Everything started to pick up.
The Old Lady bought a Blitz army truck.
This was a better ride;
No window her side.

The old lady did not complain anymore.
This was better than the old Dodge Flying Four.

A large brown snake stretched out by the door.
The Old Lady stepped back she never swore.

The snake took off across the yard.
To find him again would be hard.

Mulka Store had many holes in the walls.
The Old Lady knew the snake would be back,
He could get in through any crack.

She saw the snake come in.
After being caught;
The snake was put in the bin.

Mixing up her lime and pug,
She blocked many holes in the walls,
With this mud.

She did this every day,
Trying to keep the snakes away.

Four in the morning the dust storm would roll
in with a blast,
The Old Lady would wonder 'how long will
this last?'
At sundown, it would be gone.

Windows, doors and ceiling the dirt came in.
The Old Lady did not know where to begin.
All this dirt must break her heart.
With bucket and spade she must start.

It takes a lot of her day,
To clear this dirt away.
It's a hard life on the track.
She's a tough old lady,
This will not break her back.

The rains came; dust storms had gone at last.
The Old Lady built her new homestead.
Now to sit back and ponder the past.

My first day as a stockman was not so great.
A cow charged my horse. I fell, broke my wrist.
Off to Broken Hill with the Flying Doctor,
To get it fixed.

For six weeks in Broken Hill I did stay,
Making lots of friends while away.
Ben was a great guy,
We lost contact I don't know why.
Many friends I had in Broken Hill while young.
I still remember some.

After six weeks, my wrist mended,
My time in Broken Hill ended.

When the drovers from up north,
Started coming our way,
They could not keep;
New born calves each day.

We bought a few milking cows,
To raise calves, from the drovers.
As they kept going past,
Our herd grew fast.

Cows were milked standing in a bail.
Calves were taught to drink out of a pail.
It was not long,
Our herd became fifty head strong.

Milking cows was a tedious chore,
After the rains, I would not do it anymore.

## Sandy the Rain Maker

The Old Bushman being a bit of a wag,
Said to Sandy, 'You make it rain,
I will buy you a new swag.'
Rains came everybody was happy again.
Including Sandy; he had his new swag to claim.

He did not get his new swag.
I will cut the rain off at your boundary,
Your land will get bad.
Natterannie Sand hills are on the boundary,
That's where the next rain stopped.
Next year was another good rain,
At the boundary, it stopped again.

The Old Bushman bought Sandy his swag.
It rained. There was lots of water and grass,
Sandy the Rainmaker had his new swag at last.

How that happened I cannot explain.
The Rainmaker had done it again.

## Tom Kruse

Tom was our mailman,
He would arrive Saturday morning around nine.
If he was on time,
In the Natterannie sand hills he often got stuck,
With his old Leyland Mail Truck.

Tom was a man, who did not curse or swear,
Patiently he would dig his way out of there.
At our homestead, he would stop,
Have a billy tea and a yarn,
For us I think he had a soft spot.
'Do you need anything fixed today?'
If not, he got on his way.

With a hammer and spanner,
He could fix anything that was clear.
I called him the 'Bush Engineer'.

Passing through Mungerannie Gap,
He kept heading up the Birdsville Track.
Marree, Birdsville and back,
That was Toms' mail track.

Holidays over, I must head back.
Friday, I will meet Tom at the Marree Post Office.
Ready to go up the Birdsville Track.

The Coopers still in flood,
Must go to the top crossing,
Where the river is not so wide.
There a punt and dinghy are used,
To get to the other side.

Getting to the crossing was a sad day for me,
The punt and dinghy were not there for us to see.

'Tom, we will have to wait for somebody to come.'
'No, my boy one of us will go over.'
Tom said he could not swim.
Then I knew I must go in.

With the water level dropping,
And the river not so wide,
I knew I could swim to the other side.

With my uncanny luck,
Getting out of the water,
A Ute just pulled up.

## Stockmen and drovers

Mustering over the cattle are drafted,
Cows and calves stay home.
Fat steers go to the market.
Stockmen head to the homestead to repack,
Soon they will be on the Birdsville Track.

Fresh horses are picked just for the trip,
They know Grey Trail will bolt.
'Give him the water canteens,
That will bring him to a halt.'
'The tucker pack must have a quiet horse,
Silver is the one of course.'
'His mate Pompy has a strong back,
He can carry the dry rations pack.'

They are soon on the road,
With the mob of fats.
In a few weeks, they will see;
Marree and the railway tracks.

The cook and the horse-tailer is one chap,
It's a big job he can manage that.

Past the Natterannie sand hills they go,
Travelling ever so slow.
Into Coopers Creek at last.
Lot of coolabah trees,
Not much grass

*(continued overleaf)*

The cattle can smell water,
And head for the bore.
To manage them on a dry day is a chore.
They can stop and sulk,
This brings everything to a halt.

All too soon time has passed,
Although they have not travelled fast.
At ten miles, a day,
It does seem a long way.

Marree is soon in sight.
Does seem strange,
Cattle loading on trains,
It's mostly done at night.

The droving trip is over,
The stockmen have done their best,
They head back to the station for a rest.

The drovers settled the cattle on camp,
Stomachs full and tight,
They were ready to rest for the night.

First watch started at dark,
The horse-tailer was ready to start.
He had to be up before light,
First watch was his right.

The cattlemen were next on watch,
They would sing count and recite,
This helped get through the night.

The boss drover took last watch.
He had a good night sleep,
Fresh and ready to be on his feet.

Daylight had come at last,
Drover's horses and cattle ready to start.

Days were clear, nights cold.
'It's coming,' we were told.
Spending warm days in the sun,
Who would believe, it will come.

Lying in our swags each night,
Thinking, when will conditions be right?
The fires burning down,
Just add another log.
Next morning it was there,
Our first winter fog.

Cattle loading was finished at night.
Next morning, I will head for the store,
To have three or four ice creams maybe more.
This is the highlight of my trip,
Having all the ice creams I can fit.

Back to the cattle yards,
It's now time to pack.
Must head home with the horses,
It's a quicker trip without cattle, just a few
days up the track.

## Last of the Rustlers

The packs are light,
The horses are fast,
Just on dusk they go past.
Into the night, they go,
Where to? Nobody will know.

A light plane is coming.
The poddy dodgers take fright,
Put the packsaddles under the trees;
Out of sight.
The plane flies low and fast,
This trip may be their last.

The poddy's are mustered,
After following their tracks,
Back to the horses and put on the packs.

Then homeward bound,
Trying not to make a sound.
This is their last trip in the night,
After getting such a fright.

## Billy Brainless

'Billy, you can check the cane grass swamp,
And the lake.'
He did not get home until late.
'How green was the grass Billy?'
'Green as my gold watch Boss.'

'I will get you a new shirt Billy.'
'What colour would you like?' The Boss said.
'Any colour Boss, as long as he's red.'

Holidays have come,
Into Marree Billy will go.
Any further he does not know.

Holidays over, Boss goes back to pick up Billy,
His hat, boots and swag are gone.
'What size hat do you take Billy?'
'Don't know Boss. What's yours?'
'Six and seven-eighths.'
'Good Boss, mine is eight and nine-tens."

Billy is not very bright.
Back with the horses he is just right.

The big bay colt came into the round yard.
'Don't try to break him, it will be hard.'
'Look at him, he shows the whites of his eyes.'
'I am sure it would not be wise.'

Billy got into the round yard.
It came at him with mouth open to bite.
Billy turned around and took flight.

Two big hooves hit him on the rump.
It speared him between the round yard rails.
Billy got up feeling the pain.
The Boss said, 'let him go.'
'I don't want to see him again'.

From Australian bushmen,
Great stories are told.
Sitting around the campfire,
We wait for them to unfold.

We sneer and think they are dumb,
As for schooling, most had none.
They are clever in their own way,
Always "The Bushmen" they will stay.

## Aberdeen Angus

The black poleys are wild cattle I can say,
They come out of the lignum and gallop away.
To tell the Old Bushman, 'They are Aberdeen Angus.'
He will say, 'You are dumb;"
'They are black poleys my son.'

You must remember what I say and do,
This is going to be the life for you.
I try not to be smart and lend a hand,
This is my life on the land.

Summer was hot and dry,
Nary around but a fly.
Even snakes were too hot,
Staying in a shady spot.

Dingoes came into drink all day,
They had adjusted to this way.
Horses would come in after dark.
Have a drink then go,
Before the sun started to show.

Cattle would camp at the water all day,
Waiting for the sun to go away.
There was little grass about,
The country was heading into drought.
They could not last,
Many dying with this hot blast.

I called our place Boiling Downs.
During summer, I lost many pounds.
Every day was very hot,
Must check our waters and stock.

Not a cloud in the sky,
The rain stayed away.
We must sell stores without delay.

It's disappointing to see,
Our stock trucked out.
We must be tough,
And live with another drought.

## Jerk-a-long

The red roan gelding was called Jerkalong.
He changed stride all day long.
Very annoying to ride,
Giving me a nasty pain in the back and side.

For mustering, he was not fast.
As a result, his condition would last.
At the end of the day I unsaddled and let him go,
Feeling the pain,
Soon I will have to ride him again.

Mustering over the horses are let go.
There's Jerkalong ever so slow.
Next season I will give him another ride,
Enough time to forget,
The pain in my back and side.

They left the homestead with a mob of fats.
I caught them up with horses,
After putting on the packs.

The Old Bushman came to me,
'Guess what I forgot? Sugar and tea.'
Heading back to the homestead,
I did not take a packhorse;
Jerkalong can do the job of course.

At the homestead, I did not dither.
Putting a calico bag each side Jerkalong's wither.

One bag sugar the other tea,
Back to the cattle where I had to be.
'Sorry I was slow.'
'Don't worry.' Said the Old Bushman,
'It was Jerkalong, we all know.'

## Black Hat

Black Hat was my mate.
He was very tall,
With plenty of weight.
Getting up in the mornings he was slow.
As always waiting for the campfire glow.

He was my best cob,
Cattle tailing was his job.
He would watch them graze all day,
Not letting any stray.
We had good times until his end.
A good mate at rest.
He was one of the best.

On the road with a big mob,
We were going past Blazer's Well.
There some tourists were having a spell.
They asked me and Black Hat,
To, 'Stop for a chat?'
They had lots of questions to ask,
As the cattle kept moving past.
'What do you do with them after dark?'
'We round them up tight,'
'And watch them all night.'

One night camped at Russell's Creek,
The mozzies were so bad we could not sleep.
The bushman Old Roy,
Had a mozzie net in his swag.
He was smart in his own way,
It was bush experience I must say.
He had a good night sleep.
Next day we were out on our feet.

## Dingoes, Brumbies, and Birds

From Lake Hope to Lake Eyre,
Along Coopers Creek.
Dingoes, brumbies, and birds are there,
It's still in drought,
No grass or water about.

Dingoes are very smart,
To find water is an art.
Where the riverbanks and sand hills meet,
Water does seep.
The dingo is very wise,
When he digs in the soft sand;
Water will rise.
This allows the dingoes,
Brumbies and birds to survive.

The first old bushman I worked with,
His name was Roy;
He treated me as an equal, not a boy.
To me many things he wanted to show.
As a bushman, I had to grow.

With lots of things he put me to the test,
Learning to be a bushman I must do my best.
He had lots of stories to be told,
Some risqué, others bold.

Things he taught me made sense,
How to cook a damper or mend a fence.
To be a good horse-tailer one must know,
How to track them and find where they go.

Many more things he had to show me,
Roy the old bushman was carefree.

Many years ago, out mustering,
With an old bushman named Snow,
We had mustered a large mob.
Going past a hill called Trooper's Nob,
I asked him how the hill got its name.
He said, 'The story I am going to tell you,
Is definitely true.'
'A warrior with a spear,
Caught a trooper right there.'
'The trooper had an affair, with the warriors' wife,

The warrior cut off the trooper's nob.'
'That's the hill Trooper's Nob.'
'A plaque on top of the hill says;
"It's better to have done it and lost your nob,
Than not done it at all."
Snow did tell me a lot of stories he knew,
I doubt if any were true.

We had many calves to brand that day,
Have your pannikin of tea,
Ready to start right away.

The ropes and bronco horse were ready,
Branding irons in the fire getting hot.
It's hard work. We branded the lot.

The calves are pulled up to the bronco panel,
One at a time.
Two stockmen work on the ground,
With a leg rope each,
The calves are thrown down.

One does the ear marking,
The other uses the brand.
They do this so well,
Nobody was needed to lend a hand.

The young stockman was cocky and bold,
Many feats he wanted to uphold.
Every morning he put himself to the test,
Riding the roughest, those were the best.
Many other skills he learnt each day,
Happy in himself doing things the Bushman's way.

## Horse Mustering

From the big sand hill,
Out to Wadroo Creek.
Then up to the water courses,
A day mustering horses.

Finding them at last,
They galloped home fast.
Being fat and fresh,
We drafted off the best.

Into the round yard, they came,
Some wild others were tame.
'I dreaded the day.' I could no longer stay,
To watch my horses, gallop away.

The preacher came to our place to stay,
To me he had a strange way.
The Old Lady sat everybody down,
To tea and cake,
The preacher said, 'Wait.'
'We will pray.'
Must have his wires crossed.
I did not know what to say.

We guessed he was a strange bloke,
Waving a lantern full of smoke.
'Is he a beggar?' The Old Bushman said.
There's nothing I could say.
He would not understand a preacher's way.

'It's time for me to go,
You are all good people to know.'
The Old Lady gave him plenty of food.
I filled his car with petrol.
Wishing him all the best.
He was then off to the next station,
To be their guest.

## Dart

I broke in the black gelding,
And named him Dart.
The Boss said, 'He will be a buck jumper I know.'
Cocky and full of pride,
I will give him a ride.
He bucked so powerful and fast,
I knew I could not last.

Next time I rode him will be in the sand,
Where there is a soft place to land.
Back in the river country,
I put him to the test.
There I did ride out his best.
Then hitting him under the belly,
And on the rump,
I hit the ground with a thump.
Then getting up to try again,
The Boss said, 'No'.
He's off to the rodeo.

The ringer came down from up north,
Bragging he could ride any horse.
I put him in the yard,
With the little buckjumper called Dart,
Now we will see if he is smart.

This will put him to the test,
Dart was one of the best.
He put his foot in the stirrup iron on the near side,
He was in for one hell of a ride.

Hoisting himself on the horses back,
He gave the whip one crack.
The ringer from up north,
Landed flat on his back.

The largest stock camp I worked in,
Had one hundred and fifty horses, seventeen men.
Four horse tailers I was one of them.

One morning riding along in the dark,
Another horse tailer and I were having a chat.
He was not there when I looked around.
I went back to find him on the ground.

A tree branch hit him on the chest.
'Why didn't you yell?'
'I had the bloody wind knocked out of me;
Before I fell.'

Don't get me wrong,
I did like old Bushmen.
Most of their stories may not be true,
That's the reason I only remember a few.

Sitting around the campfire light,
Their stories pass away a pleasant night.
Must go to bed just after dark.
Being a horse-tailer every morning,
Is an early start.

Leaving camp in the dark, I cannot hear a bell ring.
The horses are all asleep.
I listen quietly for a while,
Then a bell horse shakes his head.
I hear a faint ting.
There's plenty of time,
For me to get them all in.

Maybe a few are still away,
On camp the horses will stay.
I will go straight out to get the rest.
It's the beginning of another long day,
To put the horse tailer to the test.

My name is Bobby Gaye,
I am a stockman.
I can do anything your way.

The boss said, 'He is a bit slow.'
Being family, give him a go.
With him we would have fun.
Using a little pun.

Out mustering he got lost every day,
We did not care how long he was away.
He could be seen coming with the sun at his back,
Shortly he will be at the tucker pack.

In the evenings playing his guitar,
He sung us many songs.
He had many stories to tell each night.
We knew they could not all be right.

Sorry to say you all know it's time for me to go,
We wished him all the best for his trip along the track.
Just a matter of time he will be back.

He got out of his swag just on daylight,
Every morning happy and bright.
The crows had started to 'ark-ark,'
Looking for something to eat.
Not a sound from the dingoes,
They must be asleep.

Must boil the billy for a pannikin of tea,
Living out in the sand hills,
With this horse was the place to be.
At this time, he had no set plan,
Just enjoy life on the land.

Soon the horses must go home,
During that time in the sand hills,
He did not feel alone.

Natterannie, Panderannie, Oorawillannie,
Aberdare to Lake Eyre.
This is where our cattle run.
Not a very long muster to be done.

The winds are coming,
The feed will blow away,
Mustering must start any day.

So peaceful out mustering,
Not a sound.
Just the horses and cattle around.

Mustering and drafting over,
The fat cattle will be sold.
Back to the permanent waters,
The rest must stay,
And wait for another good season,
To come our way.

Spider and Blimey came up the track,
They wanted to be stockmen.
Never been on a horse before,
Not knowing their legs and bottom would be sore.

They were not very bright.
We will take them out mustering,
Hope they will be alright.

Now you boys take these cattle,
Over three sand hills and down a big flat.
There's one lone coolabah tree,
That's where we will have the dinner pack.

Spider and Blimey moved the cattle,
Over the sand hill and out of sight.
To leave them alone would not be right,
I followed along over the next sand hill,
Where I could not be seen,
Then came this distress call;
'Help, help! We're lost.'

Was horrible to see two lads this way,
We could not have them another day.

Going past Canny Bore,
I had the greatest experience I ever saw.
About twenty Brolga's dancing,
So elegant and graceful I had to stay.
They had me so mesmerised.
I could watch them all day.

Lying in my swag that night,
Thinking of the Brolga's flying away.
Hope those lovely birds come back,
To dance on the Birdsville Track.

It was a hot dry summer,
All we had was dust.
To fluke a thunderstorm,
That would be just.

Soon we could see them rise,
Ever so slowly every day.
Hope they will come our way.

The storms have gone past.
We sit back and wonder,
How long will this dry spell last?

All asleep one night,
The camp got a hell of a fright.
Thunder so loud, lighting so bright,
Rains started the season picked up,
Nature's way of giving us some luck.

## Birdsville Track

It was a good life along the track,
All day every day just horses, cattle, and tack.
Life was parochial in so many ways,
Did not see anybody; no news for many days.

Sitting down by the campfire at night,
Deep in thought; is what I am doing right?
Wondering what the city people are doing now,
Is there something I am missing?
Should I change this? I will not allow.

No radio, only the dingoes, no other sound.
Lying in my swag at night on hard ground.
Sleep came easy after a hard long day,
This is my life there's no easy way.

My dedication to horses was so great,
I treated every one of them as a mate.
When the rains came, this was the place to be.
Wild flowers on the sand hills and flats,
Then came all the rabbits and wild cats.

It was enjoyable to watch the cattle graze,
For a while, at least, no more dusty haze.
Must have a swim in every dam,
Water does not last in this land.

During winter the back of beyond was so cold.
The pain for me was great,
I was sure I would not grow old.
A place where the seasons come and go,
This was my home a good place to know.

## Wild Horses

They came out of the hills,
Down through the water courses.
Having never seen anybody,
This mob, were the craziest wild horses.

They were black, brown and bay,
We will have them in the yard today.
Some with a roach back, others sway backs,
Many I would like to break in for hacks.

The inbreeding has been so strong,
They have been left too long.
Lots will have to go, some can stay,
My favourites were black and bay.

We put them through the drafting yard,
This enjoyed it wasn't hard.
It was great while I was young,
Now I am older it's not fun.

Mine was a hard but good life those days,
I did enjoy horses and their intricate ways.

## Brumbies

They burst out of the Cooper sand hills,
On to the stony plains.
Some with splayed hooves,
Others with long flowing manes.

The mares and foals,
Came over the last sand hill fast.
Keeping the mob together,
The stallion came last.

It's a great sight,
To see brumbies in full flight.
At the yards, some break away,
Back to the Cooper sand hills to stay.

Sitting by the camp fire well after dark,
I heard this awful noise getting closer.
Maybe it was a cough, could be a bark?
To me everything is exaggerated at night.
My heart was pounding should I move out of the light?

Will I pick up the rifle or a knife?
I was in fear of my life.
Now it was getting closer should I stay?
The noise was getting worse. I will move away.

I have heard about odd events at night.
This was the first time I had such a fright.
My mind was wondering; there could be many.
Who could circle me and attack?
Having my rifle and knife, I will fight back.
No, I will stay this is my place.
Then into the camp fire light,
Appeared a donkey with a long white face.

It was hot and dusty on the stony plain,
The dingo walked on the cattle pad.
I could almost feel his pain.

Getting to the bore,
He stood in the water.
Paws hot and sore.

The dingo would have his drink.
Then head out across the flat,
To a shady tree there he sat.

After dark the dingoes would howl,
It was a distant lonely call.
I did not know whether it was,
A happy noise or a growl.

Next morning there was not a sound.
Checking on the tracks,
I could see the dingoes had been around.

To mention the Birdsville Track,
All people think of is heat, dust, and flies.
For me, winter was the time I despised.
Inland at night everything froze.
Watching cattle, I had intense pain,
In my feet and toes.

Watch finished, back to my swag to get some sleep.
Three woollen blankets with a twelve by twelve camp sheet.
One blanket on the bottom two on the top,
With the camp sheet, I was never hot.

I will always remember the cold winter pain,
Glad to have summer back again.

The brumby stallion came from Lake Hope,
At Mulga Point the stockman caught him with
a rope.

We can only stop for one day,
Enough time to break in the stallion;
And ride him away.

He was a quiet horse to tame,
Being such a nice animal,
Bull Parny was his name.

The stockman broke him in his way.
Good memories of Bull Parny,
Are still there to this day.

The cattle trucks are heading north,
We saw them go past.
This droving trip will be the last.
The trucks are here to stay,
No more droving down our way.

In the early morning, I will miss the horse bells ring.
Lying in my swag at night.
Listening to the drovers sing.

We hear the trucks go past day and night,
Trucks are quicker this must be right.
Everybody must accept change,
And let the horses go to free range.

Driving past the water courses,
'Stop!' The Old Bushman said.
Here comes the brumby runner,
With a load of horses.

After their 'G'day,'
They sat down in the hot sun,
To drink a full bottle of rum.

Many bush yarns I heard that day,
If any were true, I could not say.
After five the sun was not so hot,
We headed for the Cooper,
To find a good camp spot.

That night the old bushman did snore.
For me I did not expect anymore.

Must take my horses for a drink,
While sitting at the bore.
I stop and think;
It's my life, should I be doing more?

To have holidays by the sea,
During hot weather,
That's where I like to be.

My friends work all day.
Am I joining in the right way?
When work is over they have their own fun.
Me, I am the odd one.

Being lonely and blue,
I will go home to Mulka,
There, I have plenty to do.

Time comes to leave the family,
I must contemplate my destiny.

# Cooper Country and More

*More verse from experiences working around Coopers Creek*

Over the flats along dusty tracks,
Past the trees, through fallen leaves,
Among the saltbush, mulga, and wattle,
This is where we go,
Sometimes stubbing a toe.

There are many things to see,
A snake or a lizard climbing a tree,
At odd times a fox will go by,
During the day, they are very shy.

The kangaroos jump up to see what's around,
After hearing any strange sound.
The conceited emu is not in a hurry,
With his head held high,
Every day he watches us go by.

Observations of all, in a day on the land,
To stay here forever what a wonderful plan.

There's little we can do during the heat,
Stay inside, drink and eat.
Winter we did not like the cold,
Now summer is here, it's worse getting old.

There are lots of people at the beach,
Some walk in the water to cool their feet.

Many lay on the sand,
Under the blazing sun getting a tan.
I feel like a sloth moving so slow,
Waiting for the intense heat to go.

There's many little chores I must do.
During hot days, I can only consider a few.
It will be sometime until the heat goes away,
I like heading down to the beach,
There I would like to stay.

He was the cooper stockman,
Many experience's in his mind.
They will be shared with all,
Now getting older its time.

The day he broke his wrist,
Along came the cook,
'Let me pull it in place,
Then it will be fixed'.

The cook had Barcoo Rot,
Was dirty to see every day,
Being an old bushman,
He cured it his way.

Covered with sticky tape,
For some days, he did wait,
When the tape came away,
No more Barcoo rot to this day.

How clever was he?
The bushman's remedy.


*'Barcoo Rot' is a Vitamin A deficiency

## Lake Hope

Heading up river to Lake Hope,
Must rely on every soak,
Stockmen, horses, and cattle,
Need water every day,
Soakage, that's the only way.

Cooper country we know,
To muster cattle that's where we go.
They come out of Lignum and Gallopaway,
Stockmen and horses tire every day.

Mustering over now head back,
There's more feed on the Birdsville Track.
It's a long way to each soak,
Walking cattle and horses from Lake Hope.
Down the river channel they go,
Head for Mulka, that's home, these cattle know.

They came up the race,
Setting a cracking pace,
Cows and calves, we know,
Bulls always slow.

Through the forcing pen,
Then the round yard,
Drafting this way and that,
Some poor, some fat.

So easy to get attached,
Many must be dispatched.
All the steers I know,
Now fat they must go.

The trucks at the loading ramp,
It's getting dark must use a lamp.
The cattle are loaded out.
Have a beer give all a shout.

## Lonely Drover

'Twas his first trip down the track,
Six fifty head strung out in line,
Heading for the next water,
They will be there by dinner time.

The drover did not have much to say,
Was lonely riding at the tail all day,
They settle the cattle down at night,
Ready to rest stomachs full and tight.

There was an old piker,
Whom took the lead,
The meanest bullock,
He would not stop to feed.

Lot of character among them all,
The drovers rode behind sitting tall.
Droving was the same every day,
The trip is over cattle trucked away.

The drover would head home,
With his packs and horses all alone.
Nobody knows where he will go,
Could be anywhere maybe Naryilco.

## Jillaroo

She did not have a skirt,
Wide brimmed hat and britches,
With a bright blue shirt.

Work and talk horses,
This she did every day,
Total dedication, was her way.

She broke them in ready to ride,
Then waited for stockmen to come by.
Some bucked others quiet,
Her skill was to be admired.

The stockmen would stay,
Hoping for her affection one day.
To her horses, she would stay true,
The smart, skilled Jillaroo.

The stockman rode off into the hot sun,
On his favourite horse,
With a water bag lunch in his saddle bag.
This work must be done.

He rode a long way,
Cattle and waters,
To check every day.

Calves bogged at a soak,
Must pull them out with a rope.
Cows he does know,
Some missing where did they go?

These are things the stockman does and knows,
Out on the run where ever he goes.

For breakfast its steak and a pannikin of billy tea,
For lunch its damper corned beef with a pannikin of billy tea,
Then comes evening, the stockmen in camp where they like to be,
With damper, hot curry, a pannikin of billy tea.

That's the Bushmen's menu every day,
The works hard, days are long.
Stockmen are hungry,
They like curry, hot tea, strong.

Then settle by the campfire light,
Tell stories late into the night.
They lie in their swags,
Reminisce what they did that day.

Mustered, drafted, branded,
That's what they did every day.

## The Jackaroo

Muster cattle, ride a horse,
Cook a damper and a stew,
A parochial life,
That's all he knew.

Nothing else to know,
Nowhere to go,
So little to say,
That's it every day.

For this day's work,
He's done his best,
Roll out the swag,
It's time to rest.

The cattle lie down,
Horses moving around,
It's a dream come true,
For the proud Jackaroo.

## Dingoes Love Song

The dingo stood on the sand hill,
Howling at the moon.
Was it a call for a partner?
To meet him soon?

There were other dingoes around,
Making that eerie sound,
Could be mating time? Who's to say,
A friendly love song? Come out to play?

After sundown, they start,
Wild calls in the dark.
Feeding time is at night.
When they are alert and bright.

Catching rabbits, mice, and rats,
Over sand hills, down stony flats.
When it comes to day light,
They settle down from a long night.

Now to sleep, all day long,
Was it the dingoes love song?
That we cannot say.

## Cold Breaker

The Stockman bragged,
He could break in any horse,
With halter and bag of course.

This he did for many a long day,
Then came the Shetland pony,
With a different way.

The stockman had no hope,
After catching the pony with a rope.
Throwing itself on the ground,
There it would stay,
Until the rope was taken away.

For many a day, this was the same,
The Shetland pony he could not tame.
The stockman did not brag anymore,
Memories of the little pony he keeps in store.

Wild turkey, dingoes, and birds,
So much to see,
That's Cooper's Creek.
Where I like to be.

The flood runs down,
Water holes full,
Yellow belly and brim,
These fish abound.

Had good times on Cooper's Creek.
Catching fish is a treat,
There I like to be,
Camped under a Coolabah tree.

They built their own cattle yards,
With Cooper's Creek Coolabahs,
Post think and strong.
Rails wide and long.

Big on the bottom,
Ten inch at the top,
With axe and adze,
They cut the lot.

To load to the truck,
Over a tree branch,
A rope was slung,
To lift them one by one.

Thirty posts a day,
Cut them load them,
Travel to the new yards.
Many miles away.

Was hard work every day.
Building yards in the hot sun.
Now it's finished.
The stockmen smiled. It', all done.

## Cooper Dreamer

The stockman came from up north,
Time to forget swag and horse.
Bush fly's and dusty days,
Now to change his ways.

Cattle and horses still in mind,
His way will change, in time.
Looking to the north,
Wondering, 'Where is my horse'?

Day's work over, go home to tea,
With his camp oven and damper.
In the Cooper sand hills
That's where he wants to be.

Forever memories will stay,
Life on the Cooper,
Was his way.

It was a long way home,
He walked slowly alone.
Not noticing what was around.
All day walking over hot ground.

His feet would be hurting,
His legs tired,
He met some mates under a shady tree.
Not stopping, home, he wanted to be.

Over sand hill's, across flats,
My favourite horse,
Had broken hobble straps.

Campsite was Saltbush Creek,
The saltbush stood six feet.
A difficult camp spot.
We could not see the lot.

Cattle rounded up tight,
'T was a very dark night,
First watch came and went.

Next watch, little sound,
Were cattle moving around?
Then came lightning so bright,
Cattle were seen out feeding all night.

So embarrassing to say,
We were watching saltbush,
Never told anybody to this day.

Shorthorn and Hereford,
Breeds we know,
In the Cooper country,
They will grow.

Out in the sand hills,
With buck-bush and paddymelon,
They need, little water
Fattening on good feed.

A long way from water they could go,
Chasing paddymelons, the track riders know.
Tracking them every day,
Near water they must stay.

When the paddymelons dry,
They head back to water.
Thanks to the track riders,
Nary one did die.

From the Cooper to home,
With a mob of cattle and his horse,
The stockman rode alone.

Must keep moving all night,
Before the sun rises hot and bright.
Cattle kept walking without a sound,
'Twas a dark night, nothing around.

Soon the sun will be in the sky,
Too hot to move cattle.
With this heat, some could die.

The cattle smell water,
They head for the bore.
The stockman had a good night.
Travelled twenty miles or more.

## Rabbits Galore

The meat chillers were there,
Trappers were everywhere,
On the sand hills and flats,
All setting traps.

Rabbits galore,
Most I ever saw.
Lots yellow, others grey,
Biggest plague to this day.

They were trapped, netted and shot.
No way to catch the lot.
Summer came, little feed about,
Conditions did wipe them out.

## Cooper Country

Horses are thirsty,
The soaks dry,
Sand hills are hot.
No shade to stop.

Next soak's a long way,
Must keep moving all day.
Digging soak's in the hot sun,
Horses thirsty, must be done.

Next soak waters there,
For dingoes and birds,
Plenty to share.

Where the river channel,
And sand hills meet.
Soaks are there,
That's Cooper's Creek.

## Stampede

The moon was up high,
Not a cloud in the sky.
Cattle moving around,
Horses skittish, not a sound.

The cattle rushed off into the night,
With haste, out of sight.
The noise I still remember now,
As they went past,
Every steer and cow.

Tracked them next day,
They went a long way.
Why did they go?
The stockmen did not know.

Spinifex on the sand hills,
Red gibbers on the plains,
Bull-rushes in the water,
Along the bore drains.

That's where the dingoes roam,
With brumbies and birds its home,
Cane-grass in the swamps, many feet high,
Abundant with water birds to espy.

Needle bush trees in the sand hills,
Where eagles nest,
So peaceful hardly a sound.
Animals resting on soft ground.

The silence is broken when a crow flies by,
With his noisy ark, ark, in the sky.
The dingo woke to a strange sound,
He slunk away over hot ground,
To a quiet spot, he would stay,
Resting to the end of the day.

The outback is alive,
Animals, birds, and insects,
Summer and winter all survive.

There were wildflowers on the sand hills,
Mitchell grass on the plains.
'Twas the best of summer rains.

Wild turkeys in the river country,
Most I ever saw.
Flocks of a hundred or possibly more.

Grasses three feet high,
Only time to see turkeys,
When they rose in the sky.

Then comes Spring time,
Birds nesting on the ground,
Along the water's edge,
Dingo pups, running around.

The Cooper floods into Lake Eyre,
Takes some time to get there,
What great country up the Birdsville Track,
Next good season, let's go back.

## Wild Brumby Mare

Dark shiny brown,
Some would say black,
Never to be a hack.

One club hoof,
A long, tangled mane,
She galloped across the plain.

The wildest mare,
I ever saw,
Came to drink,
At Mulka Bore.

After a drink, she would not stay,
So flighty, looked every which way,
The wild mare, we left alone,
Out in the sand hills was her home.

They came down the track,
'Twas a jeep and a truck,
In the sand both got stuck.
The sand hills called Oldfield's Leap,
They were destined to meet.

During the heat of the day,
That's where they had to stay,
They rested until the sand was cold,
Let down your tyres, they were told.

Unload the truck until the weight is light,
May take all night.
'Twas a frustrating job.
Only way to get out of the bog.

Early next day,
The truck could get away,
Then to reload,
A day lost on the road

*Oldfield's Leap was a big sand hill between
Coopers Creek and Mulka Station

The stockman was sad,
This he could not say.
No more Cooper country,
'Twas his last day.

Going through Cooper's Creek,
If only he could weep,
On past Blazer's Well,
Many stories to tell.

Brolga's dancing at Canny Bore.
If black hat was here,
He could tell you more,
His memory will stay,
With the stockman every day.

Cattle and horses in the past,
This trip is the last.
Down the Birdsville Track,
There's no looking back.

He walked up and down Pt. Patterson Road,
Deep in thought.
Remembering the old bushmen,
And the life he was taught.

South of the dingo fence he would stay,
Never to forget the old busman's way.
He was thinking of his curry damper;
And pannikin of billy tea.
Now much older, this is the place he must be.

Still fit and well,
There were many stories.
He had to tell,
Mostly true I must say,
With fiction, he does not have a way.

*A Note from the Author*

*Many times, I have been asked to write about
my life and experiences living on the Birdsville
Track.
I have been contemplating doing this for a
long time.
To me, my story has a lot more character
written in verse.
This is a condensed version of events; I hope
you have enjoyed reading my book.*

*I must commend my partner, Raelene Hill.
Raelene encouraged me to write my book
now.
Her greatest attribute has been helping me
with verses - and tolerant listening.
Reminds me of the adage: 'Patience is a virtue
often found in women'.*


*Peter Daw
A Cattleman of South Australia
2016*

www.ingramcontent.com/pod-product-compliance
Lightning Source LLC
Chambersburg PA
CBHW031428290426
44110CB00011B/566